# The Bone Saw Café

### POETRY FROM THE HEART

BY: MIKE BROWN

**Gotham Books**

30 N Gould St.
Ste. 20820, Sheridan, WY 82801
https://gothambooksinc.com/

Phone: 1 (307) 464-7800

© 2025 *Mike Brown*. All rights reserved.

No part of this book may be reproduced, stored in a retrieval system, or transmitted by any means without the written permission of the author.

Published by Gotham Books (May 13, 2025)

ISBN: 979-8-3493-3522-8 (P)
ISBN: 979-8-3493-3523-5 (E)

Because of the dynamic nature of the Internet, any web addresses or links contained in this book may have changed since publication and may no longer be valid.

The views expressed in this work are solely those of the author and do not necessarily reflect the views of the publisher, and the publisher hereby disclaims any responsibility for them.

# Table of Content

(The Bone Saw Cafe) .................................................................. 1

(Belinda) ...................................................................................... 2

(Danielle) ..................................................................................... 3

(Robbery of time) ........................................................................ 4

(The Vines) .................................................................................. 5

(Late) ............................................................................................ 6

(The leaves of the heart) ............................................................. 7

(The Gates) .................................................................................. 8

(The Green Shed) ........................................................................ 9

(Gear Jammers (101)) ............................................................... 10

(The Hero) ................................................................................. 11

(The Blue Walls) ....................................................................... 12

(The Black Cross) ..................................................................... 13

(The Church) ............................................................................. 14

(Big Pink) .................................................................................. 15

(The Darkness with in) ............................................................. 16

(No teeth not one) ..................................................................... 17

(The wig) ................................................................................... 18

(The payless man) ..................................................................... 19

(The Bridge) .............................................................................. 20

(Texting Ghost) ......................................................................... 21

(The Source) .............................................................................. 22

(Existing in time) ...................................................................... 23

(The Sliver) ................................................................................ 24

(The Mail) .................................................................................... 25
(Butterfly in the sand) ................................................................. 26
(The Darkest Hour) ..................................................................... 27
(The Chime) ................................................................................ 28
(The lines of summer) ................................................................. 29
(The song and the river) .............................................................. 30
(A knock at the door) .................................................................. 31
(The Dust) ................................................................................... 32
(The Sunlight) ............................................................................. 33
(A girl named Bee) ..................................................................... 34
(So much food) ........................................................................... 35
(The four helium balloons) ......................................................... 36
(The old shoe of time) ................................................................ 37
(Ghostly reminders) .................................................................... 38
(The stool) .................................................................................. 39
(The Tanned Ghost) .................................................................... 40
(The paper boys are on strike) .................................................... 41
(The pain sets in) ........................................................................ 42
(The serpent is my brother) ........................................................ 43
(A piece in writing) .................................................................... 44
(Thy mouth) ................................................................................ 45
(We were on the rays of the sun) ................................................ 46
(The hand of many hearts) ......................................................... 47
(The black blood) ....................................................................... 48
(The man from jubilee) .............................................................. 50
(The greatest man) ..................................................................... 51

(Snow in the desert) .................................................................... 52
(Love) ............................................................................................ 53
(The mountain) ............................................................................. 54
(These words) .............................................................................. 55
(Please write another) ................................................................. 56
(The dark horse) .......................................................................... 57
(The sound man) .......................................................................... 58
(The round table) ......................................................................... 59
(The cats stare) ............................................................................ 60
(The death of me) ........................................................................ 61
(The Jeffersons had a airplane) .................................................. 62
(The eyes) ..................................................................................... 63
(A trip to the moon) ..................................................................... 64
(The ship) ..................................................................................... 65
(The winding road) ...................................................................... 66
(Breathing) ................................................................................... 67
(E. T. ate my lasagna) ................................................................. 68
(The last poem) ............................................................................ 69

This book called (The Bone Saw Cafe) Poetry from the heart I have written from my heart and may others do the same by all means that they have available.

(Michael A. Brown)

2024

## (The Bone Saw Cafe)

There I was just going along whispering to myself. The stains from another time as years gone by. The pain of amputations of the souls of many who were insane with the fragments of life. With the pages of time washing away.

By: Mike Brown

2024

## (Belinda)

Her hair color of the midnight sun. Heart of gold but soft as a white cloud in the blue sky. I have seen her sadness. I have seen her madness and her love for the children she brought to this earth. May god in heaven always lead her forward in her path to come.

By: Mike Brown

## (Danielle)

Her hair like a river of honey. Eyes glisten like oceans waves with sun on top. Walking as flowers grow with every foot step. And butterflies move through oceans of time.

By: Mike Brown

**(Robbery of time)**

When holding on to the past. You rob today. And if you hold on to this day to tight you are stealing from the future to be.

By: Mike Brown

## (The Vines)

The vines of thirty years were tore away. As was the darkness that now the light comes in from the other side. A man and woman is sometimes cloaked in darkness till the vines of despair be be removed from thou heart •

By: Mike Brown

## **(Late)**

I am late for today. I am melting the plastic together and now, it is pretty. Like a river when the sun is going down in the winter time. I hear the time going away.

By: Mike Brown

**(The leaves of the heart)**

Leaves of time. Leaves of deceit. Leaves of -

happiness. Leaves of departure. Leaves of -

friendship. Leaves of winter time and years -

gone by •

By: Mike Brown

**(The Gates)**

From the furthest hills of Greece the gates - swing. From a spiritual ghost with a open relationship with Jesus and the father above.

By: Mike Brown

### (The Green Shed)

The white door caves in. A toilet on the side. The weeds grow tall. Bricks to the side. A bird on a hot roof simmer in the sun. He passed in the room and left this world behind.

By: Mike Brown

**(Gear Jammers (101))**

Gear jammers sledge hammers. Fifty tons of beds. Breaker (1-9) holes in the roads. Construction ahead. Roll on gear jammers.

By Mike Brown

**(The Hero)**

As the hero said. When the knife turns shake -

hands with all of them.


By: Mike Brown

**(The Blue Walls)**

The walls of blue where many come and the sound of deliverance is at hand. A mystic thought as things slip away.

By: Mike Brown

### (The Black Cross)

Not of this day. It is not one that is unholy.
With the door shutting. There is not a shadow
of any sort. But rest assured you may never
know.

By: Mike Brown

**(The Church)**

The church the boards turning grey. The leaves creeping in the open door. A book on a shelf - that goes from one corner to the other. A time faded ribbon on the dried flowers scattered about.

By: Mike Brown

## (Big Pink)

The pink haired girl would sail the oceans with her friends Eternity and Monkey while the stars would fall all around. Eternity and Monkey would have love in their eyes.

By: Mike Brown

**(The Darkness with in)**

The darkness with in is never behind. It's around in the shadows of the corners ahead. The hair of darkness with light on top. The minutes click by in red. The roots in the ground will run forever •

By: Mike Brown

**(No teeth not one)**

Had no teeth not one. Couldn't eat steak

only jello.


By: Mike Brown

## (The wig)

The wig of fake identity. Two people in one body. How the two people move about as one. Fighting for the one to be the dominate of the two.

By: Mike Brown

**(The payless man)**

A shoe he has only one. A sock with a hole. The shoe is green. A blue towel hangs on the grill. A spill on the floor. A pipe layer blisters in the sun with love in his eyes •

By: Mike Brown

## (The Bridge)

In between a father and his children. There is a bridge that time and death cannot shatter. Each stand at one end needing to cross and meet. The bridge I mention is your love for your father.

By: Mike Brown

**(Texting Ghost)**

I text the living but get no response. Am I texting a mime. What are the ghost doing maybe having a beer. Or having some cool beans. Do the ghost need a vitamin.

By: Mike Brown

## (The Source)

The source of everything has a beginning. What is the source? Where is the source for it all? Do stars have a source in the sky • Can every one sees the source? The source of Jesus. The - source of judgement. The source of the heart or the end of a light burning bright.

By: Mike Brown

## (Existing in time)

A sliver of existence from the start of time. The land falls to nothing. The home of emptiness is all around. The hand of time is turning red. The water is on the blade. The heart is fading away. He stands without a vision of things to be.

By: Mike Brown

**(The Sliver)**

The sliver of glass falls under the time with the foot hills of our departure. The waves wash away the underside of my time away. The time the heart breaks away as the wind blowing up from the east. As the sails break away. First and beyond.

By: Mike Brown

## (The Mail)

The mail of yesterday came today. And the mail of today will come another day. Cars roll by all night. A light is on in a field in the distance for all the - buss to see. The red flags go up for tomorrow and the days to come.

By: Mike Brown

**(Butterfly in the sand)**

Today on the beach. I came across a injured butterfly. So hard to see in the sand with the blue sky above. An act of kindness from me not so busy day. I moved the butterfly into a safe sanctuary of bushes with leaves. Maybe for his final days.

By: Mike Brown

## (The Darkest Hour)

It was the darkest hour of a September night. A creature in flight. A bell in a distance. A sweet smell of blossoms along a purple fence with the moon looking down from above. The noises heard in the distance of the night creatures brought a chill through the air of silence. As day light spread over the entire world.

By: Mike Brown

**(The Chime)**

The chime of the bell. The mist would just remain on the grass. There was a memory of the two lovers in their youth being robbed from time. And just moving in the opposite direction.

By: Mike Brown

**(The lines of summer)**

The lines run long with the sheets attached. The children run through the grass. Birds in the trees. And flowers blooming with the slightest breeze all around.

By: Mike Brown

## (The song and the river)

The song rolls on as the river flows forward as the organ playing its tune. The books are not noticed and left behind. Soon people see what could have been. And the song flowing like the river.

By: Mike Brown

**(A knock at the door)**

A knock at the door. I look and no one is ever there. The old piano in the corner playing a creepy screeching tune. The knock on the door maybe from the past, present or future. Maybe the knocking coming out from my dreams of my soul.

By: Mike Brown

## (The Dust)

The dust blows down the street. It blocks my view of the past. It hides in the corners of the - world. It clings to the walls like shadows in the light going here and there. And the leaves of the seasons falling gently to the ground. Waiting on winter to come.

By: Mike Brown

**(The Sunlight)**

The sunlight on the rose-colored mirror. Reflecting in her soft green lovely eyes. Her eyes are a gift from the heavens above.

By: Mike Brown

**(A girl named Bee)**

There was a girl named Bee. Who loved the number three. Not one, two, but three. Had a child and named it (Three Walker).

By: Mike Brown

### (So much food)

So much food not enough time. Not as much food still got time. Food almost gone. The time is dragging on. The food is not really gone. And the second hand moving forward with no return.

By: Mike Brown

### (The four helium balloons)

The four helium balloons really fly away in the sky. Higher and higher they went. further and further away. My balloons travels through time. They will always travel in a memory of my life.

By: Mike Brown

## (The old shoe of time)

I noticed a old shoe on a shelf. A child's shoe.

The shoe only remaining only as one. The shoe

old brown and dusty still remains on the shelf.

And still the shoe travels through time just like

you and I.


By: Mike Brown

**(Ghostly reminders)**

As ghostly reminders go, we are reminded of who we were and where we came from but in the end we may never know.

By: Mike Brown

**(The stool)**

Will the real stool please stand up this is your life.


By: Mike Brown

**(The Tanned Ghost)**

A ghost went to a tanning bed because he was

as white as a sheet.


By: Mike Brown

**(The paper boys are on strike)**

The paper boys are on strike. The bike tires are going flat. The chains are turning to rust. The noises of the papers landing on the door steps have faded to none. To see this again have come and gone.

By: Mike Brown

## (The pain sets in)

I slept as the expanding flesh grows. The brace gets tighter. The pain grows every night. I'm scared to sleep not knowing the outcome of a new day to begin. Not knowing of maybe it is a torture of getting older. The sadness of my heart. It aches to fill a void. Not knowing how and when. It has been so long. The void is as big as the oceans at night. With not to see any - thing as the void grows beyond repair.

By: Mike Brown

## (The serpent is my brother)

His path is his own. He is a square peg in a round hole. His words is like broken glass in my heart. His way of thinking is like a supreme pizza with a dusting of crumbs and calls it crust. A step in side direction. And only looking to the middle and never straight ahead. The serpent is my brother •

By: Mike Brown

**(A piece in writing)**

The solitude of the soul-less dancer as the black clouds roll in. A black dog howling in the morning sun. The crows have taken flight. As a stench from below call them to come and savor the meals that awaits.

By: Mike Brown

## (Thy mouth)

Out of thy mouth. Imaginary fragments of shattered glass and fumes of darkness and the damage of dreams that as far away as a bottom - less pit of decay and darkness. With a slight gleam of light as it pushes down all the cold of rage and desire. And tears flowing down like lava from a volcano one hundred miles wide.

By: Mike Brown

## (We were on the rays of the sun)

We were on the rays of the sun. We ate a syrup sandwich. And drank chocolate milk. We listened to the birds that were flying by. Hey I think we forgot the suntan lotion. Hey is there any bacon?

By: Mike Brown

## (The hand of many hearts)

The hand of many hearts as it comes down to the result of touch. As between two lovers who share a walk of enjoying the sunlight inside their hearts. And then as the moonlight shines down on the hand of many hearts a love has awoke. The hand of many hearts from the beginning of time has evolved from everything and everyone in all the corners of the world. Me my - self and my own hand of many hearts is broken and shattered into a river of shadows and sadness. Which I have not been able to repair. And now as I write this poem, poetry and art is all I can possess and carry forward through my second part of life. And my tears flow on the inside of my heart.

By: Mike Brown

## (The black blood)

The black blood came out of the ground were the heart had been buried. Ethan had to look. And right then a huge black dog coming out of the woods charging. It had no fear of Ethan. Ethan remembering something in his pocket • But the only thing he found in his pocket was lent and dirt. The dog started to drank the black blood and going crazy. Possession had over taken its body. Growling, barking, foaming at its mouth Ethan scared for his life ran deep into a big cave. It seemed to be the home of the dog. Not knowing what had happened the dog began to chase Ethan into the cave. He saw Ethan. By now Ethan was very upset. He knelt down. With the dog com - ins closer and closer so vicious he was. Ethan noticed some cupcakes. Ethan gave them to the dog. That made the dog very happy. So much so all the anger and hatred came pouring out of its body. Must have been magic cupcakes. So, Ethan and his new dog ran off together. (The End)

By: Mike Brown

## (The man from jubilee)

The man from jubilee arrived by train to the tiny town of Castle Burg. He was very concerned about the people who were watching him. Like he was something that fell out of the sky. Straight from nowhere. Why were the eyes focused on him. Was he a spy they thought. A lunatic from down the road. Soon he drifted away. The people would never know.

By: Mike Brown

**(The greatest man)**

The greatest man is nobody.


(By: Mike Brown)

**(Snow in the desert)**

I went to the desert on a field trip. While in the desert it started to get really cold and started to snow. The sand got as hard as bricks. Suddenly out of the distance came the sun and heat melting the snow and ice it soon turned into rivers and waterfalls soon flowers and trees took growth at a enormous rate. The butterflies came. And the birds flew by. It was a gift from Jesus. Just like this poem.

By: Mike Brown

**(Love)**

Love can't be measured until the hour of

departure.

By: Mike Brown

**(The mountain)**

The mountain is beautiful with snow. But after its losses its snow green grows from underneath. In every loss is a gain as in every gain is a loss.

By Mike Brown

### (These words)

These words are evolving. These words are dissolving into the wind. To try to blow under another raised window. As for waiting on the next rain storm that is coming with no appointment or apology •

By: Mike Brown

## (Please write another)

Please write another song, another poem.

Another letter to a lost love, a lost friend.

To yourself as a reminder to go ahead instead

of just setting in one place. Another to your

pet. Or another to your beloved wife or husband

or kids. (Please write another)


By: Mike Brown

## (The dark horse)

The dark horse of the lost forest. Only certain people could see the horse. The loudness of its feet pounding in the rain was deadly to hear. With the dark horse running about and flames pouring out of its nostrils people living in the lost forest never ventured far from home. Especially not knowing what reaction of the dark horse and their demise.

By: Mike Brown

**(The sound man)**

A sound man not advancing himself he endlessly becomes himself. Every man has his yes and no.

By: Mike Brown

**(The round table)**

Upon the round table is where the bones are bare. And toucans sit on each side. A light standing behind. Pointing down. The umbrella so tall under the sky of giant clouds. The round table sees and knows all and stands alone

By: Mike Brown

## (The cats stare)

The cats stare like a look of love but on the beastly look of torture from all whom shy away from such gentle creatures. And full of claws and teeth and wisdom and having god awful scream - ins all through the night as calls of satanic vibes. From sexual relationships of not ever having love for not many of the partners. And never a honey - moon or well I guess they might have vows. As ones tail sticking up to its back strutting its stuff.

By: Mike Brown

## (The death of me)

The death of me I was on a table of cold steel. I was not there I saw the bodies of light on one side and the bodies of darkness in the other corner of the room with what seemed to be a stench of hatred and betrayal cloaking their existence. With fire and torment coming from the place were the bodies of darkness stood as I knew nothing about my past life. My new life had begun and then the bodies of light moved in on me devoirs me with love and a feeling of - (conclusion # 32)

of peace. We drifted away together and so leaving the bodies of darkness and so a new journey for me to discover and I will live forever.

By: Mike Brown

## (The Jeffersons had a airplane)

The Jeffersons had a airplane. The Jeffersons would sometimes go flying. The Jeffersons airplane only had one seat. The left wing was gone the airplane had a stick with a few green leaves on the stick for the wing. The plane was green and white with a black stripe on the door. The sticks would fall on its roof. As the sticks we're waging war against the machine. And with the white rabbit deep inside and frightened of the world beyond the Jefferson's airplane.

By: Mike Brown

**(The eyes)**

Sometimes maybe it's the eyes that blind a man because he can see but doesn't look.

By: Mike Brown

## (A trip to the moon)

We left this world to go to the moon. Soon we were flying through the air at fifty thousand miles in a second. Once there we noticed a lemonade stands. The stand said made in a flash on the side. Unfortunately, it was closed for the Christmas holiday.

By: Mike Brown

## (The ship)

The ship drifted across the black sea as like to be pushed by a force from another planet. IS lights dim but visible. As the waves slamming against the door of the rooms below. A faint sound from a bell could be heard. The ships voyage would be wrapped in history with iB own fate waiting its disposal as the years faded away.

By: Mike Brown

## (The winding road)

He traveled the dark winding road for years. As not to be surprised of the unknown. And then it stood in the middle of the road. A black mass with a faceless body with arms outward. A mass darker than the darkness that surrounded its body.

Scared he would never stop. For the terrible feelings now in his mind. To never be seen again.

By; Mike Brown

## (Breathing)

To breath. To see our lust in the eyes of her. To feel a section to connect a portion of control in one inch of our life. We breath the heart beats strong and soon a weakness gripping our soul. A shutter a flutter of passion. The ashes of deceit of darkness. And with the washing away of time as to bring forth a new life that comes through a new series of happiness. As the end drives on.

By: Mike Brown

### **(E. T. ate my lasagna)**

He ate my lasagna. He didn't ask. His space ship radar was set on take it and fly away. Now I am hungry.


By: Mike Brown

**(The last poem)**

The last poem the streak is over. Not a thought came to mind. The visions from his heart were no more. Where did it all go. Maybe gone with a gust of wind. Maybe back to heaven where the words came from. I will never know. The only answer is well maybe you know the answer.

By: Mike Brown

This book called: The Bone Saw Cafe is poetry from my heart written in a really short time. I hope for anyone who reads my thoughts it brings joy to your life. And maybe my thoughts will travel on with your thoughts from my thoughts and creativity.

THE BONE SAW CAFE
2024 Poetry from the HEART 2024

By Mike Brown

www.ingramcontent.com/pod-product-compliance
Lightning Source LLC
LaVergne TN
LVHW061040070526
838201LV00073B/5130